New Days

A Collection of Poems

Anne McManus

First Published 2019
Frank Fahy Publishing Services
5 Village Centre
Barna, Galway
Ireland
www.frank-fahy.com

Cover photograph:
Lough Corrib from Oughterard, Co. Galway
© 2019 Frank Fahy
All rights reserved.

ISBN: 9781084198685

Dedication

This collection is dedicated to my husband
Ray, our children, Paul, David, Grainne and
Claire, and to our twelve grandchildren, all of
whom have brought me much love, joy and
pleasure and made me what I am.

Contents

Introduction

While I never thought of myself as a writer, throughout my long life I have somehow managed to notice those moments which make me stop and think; these can be funny, quirky, poignant, breath-taking, mysterious and often beautiful.

September in Rathanoragh

The red thrasher came
In early September to our lane.
Sun-tanned men wielded pitchforks,
Magic wands,
Tossing the yellow sheaves high
In the easy rhythm of the ritual.

The stripping of grain from straw
Bettered any magician's tricks,
The steady flow of gold,
The pulsing of the machine,
The smell of oats and wheat.

The tea came in five naggin bottles
Sweetened and milked,
Wrapped in the *Sligo Champion*,
Rasher sandwiches in batch bread.

The men sat against the bulging sacks
And murmured among themselves.
Some smoked.
Then Dan Calway's heavy boot
Crushed a field mouse into the stubble,
Staining it red,
Killing my innocence.

Normal Rules Don't Apply

It began in a yoga class;
The lean instructor urging us gently,
Stretch, stretch, sway, sway,
Hoooo–ld the breath, re–lax.

Breathe into the abdomen,
Into the chest, into the upper chest, release
slowly;
Breathe into each pose.

Week three – the cat.
On all fours – arch back on inhalation,
Lower back, raise chest on exhalation;
Stronger, stronger, buttocks in the air.
Relax.

Week four – I like being a cat.
I stretch out like elastic,
Sinuous, crouching.
I begin to purr; my ears twitch.
Exhale, relax, purr, purr.

Week five – my nails grow long,
Fingers splayed; eyes narrowed
Waiting to pounce.

I am a cat.

Relax, Mr Instructor,
Relax.

Homage to a Winter Garden

The earth lies weary
Wreathed in tangled afterbirth.
Ungratefully I scowl through my kitchen
window
At the dank, dormant soil
Momentarily forgetting
The abundance of its unselfish energy.
Just a few tenacious roses cling to a dripping
stem
To make me wonder.
I reproach myself for my ingratitude;
A mother should know better.
I vow to feed the soil;
But – not just now
In these November days;
My momentary gratitude
Does not extend to suffering.
Yet, before the certainty of winter
I have already turned the soil
To bed the bulbs in anticipation of renewal.

Such presumption can scarcely be forgiven
While I hibernate on an annual promise.
Across the evergreen hedge
The lowered sunlight shafts through the
kitchen window,
Casting its uncertain light on the fridge door.
My own solstice,
A sure sign of winter
And a welcome breakfast guest.

Irish Hedonism

Neither the nuclear bomb,

The troubles in the North,

Nor Bishop Casey being a human father

Changed our mindset.

It was one word –

Pamper.

Wrap yourself in seaweed, in tinfoil, steam for

an hour;

Indian, Turkish, Thai – have a massage.

Buy exclusive chocolates, exotic fruits, full

bodied wines,

On line.

Pamper yourself at a luxury spa

In the heart of the Burren.

Above all – indulge.

Remember – it's your right

To feel good.

Never mind the cost,

Wave the gold card

In their eager faces.

From Estonia to Ballintubber Abbey

They sit in a circle of candlelight
Around the simple altar.
Harmony
In this ancient place of worship;
Whitewashed walls,
Unadorned arches,
Slender windows,
Stillness.

From nowhere comes a sound,
Floating, in search of a resting place
Until it settles on our ears;
Voices gradually forming, layer on layer,
Arvo Part's* Hymn of Repentance.
I am subsumed into cosmic sound,
Hoping for redemption.

*Arvo Part is an Estonian composer

Goodbye

The mantra of goodbyes
Seal the unshed tears
In the labyrinth of my heart,
As deep as any unspoken thought.
Attempting to be strong,
Wearing a camouflaging smile,
I postpone my sadness
During those crucial minutes.
Or have I got it wrong?
Are swollen eyes and wet cheeks
Expected as a sure sign of love
At the departure gate?
How can they know
That when I least expect it,
Often in a happy moment,
The lid explodes off my tears
And I remember too much.

Emptiness

Emptiness cruelly confounds our fragile
spirits.
Empty house,
Empty bed,
Empty arms,
Empty heart,
Bring daunting desolation.
But witness the empty tomb:
An apparent catastrophe;
Silently heralding victory over death,
Terrifyingly unexpected,
Testing trust to the limit.

Falling Apart

I'm beginning to disintegrate.
I've noticed it a lot of late.
My hair is starting to get thin,
I'm developing a double chin.
My body is in awful freefall,
The boobs, the belly, worst of all.
My eyes and ears are getting weak,
And God! My bladder has begun to leak.
The dentist says my teeth are rotten,
Crowns and implants best forgotten.
The best things now are shiny gnashers
To grind the chops, the spuds and rashers.
My pelvic floor is quickly slipping,
My heavy breasts need tuck and nipping.
Too late for Botox, I'll detox
With castor oil, and coffee enema.
I'm on the horns of a dilemma.
But wait, there's hope – all is not lost,
Though lots of euros it will cost.
I've seen the ad, next week I'll go
Where I can be rejuvenated.

They'll wrap me up in roasted dung

From my nipples, bells will be hung.

Then concentrated cow's placenta

Mixed with geranium magenta

Will be given me to drink.

I hope to God I won't get sick.

Two hours then to lie and steam.

I wake up from a lovely dream,

Wrinkle free, a brand new me.

But when I look into the glass,

I'm still the same, óchón, alas.

Two hundred euros down the drain,

I won't get caught like that again.

Bog Walk

The throb of a pile-driver forebodes
The scarring of the landscape
To meet the needs of the house-hungry
In the face of galloping inflation
And the flamboyant confidence of the Minister
for Finance.

Unsurpassed views, only two remaining
In this exclusive development,
The gaudy billboard purrs
To seduce the desperate, the tasteless, the
opportunist
In the shortest possible time.

Boulders, forged by the force of glacial shifts,
Are tossed aside;
Bog land mesh ripped apart
By bright yellow diggers
Operated by mechanical men
Certain of their wage packets.

In the distance, the sea gleams
Under the bulk of Black Head:
A pure sky arches over the Aran Islands,
All seems normal.
But the music of the bog is silenced forever.

Chocolate

Chocolate melts at body temperature;

Endorphins, and serotonin

Lurk in its depths

Waiting to seduce us.

'Chocolate is an aphrodisiac,'

Purrs the therapist on the radio.

'Good for those with heart disease

And the darker the better.'

At last, I can enjoy my nightly bar,

Guilt free.

Christmas

His glassy eyes,
His hairy hump, his lumpy feet,
His thick curled lips
Made my childhood Christmas.
One camel among three.
Did they take turns, the Magi,
Or toss a coin?
I longed to get into his saddle,
Grasp the embroidered reins in my ten-year-
old hands.
That year, on a quiet January day,
I stole out of our bright kitchen,
Into the nearby, dim cathedral,
Climbed into the leather saddle,
And rode that camel to the Orient,
Following the star.

Concerto

Sensuous hands hover, waiting.

Coming to life, they caress the keys,

Releasing a complex mesh of sound

Which flows into my tired spirit.

Nothing exists outside that melodic flow.

Notes fade in a final coda.

Seconds of silence, applause.

The return to reality shocking.

The listening – sheer heaven.

Digital

Foxgloves, *(Digitalis),* ornamental, medicinal;
Deadly poisonous, we were told,
So we would not shove our fingers into the
blooms.
But we did anyway; the pollen a giveaway.

Then Digital came to our town.
Nothing botanic about it,
Making computers as big as washing
machines.
Rents rose, coffee shops mushroomed, money
flowed.
Two decades on,
Everyone tapping frantically.
Mobiles, iPads, smart phones.
Minimal eye contact.
It's all in the fingers these days

A Stranger

For years I knew myself, my place and where I
fitted.
Energy flowed unhindered.
Life was good.

Then, I was lost to others,
But mostly to myself.
A stranger in a dark, lonely place.
I was inside out;
Vulnerable and sensitised.

Later, redeeming light pierced the shroud,
Bit by bit
Taking its time
Until, one day, I met and recognised myself.

Coney Island, Co Sligo, September 1978

On Carty's strand, at the west end of the
island,
We are in another world
Unchanged by time.
We pick dillisk
For my great uncle Tom.
Luke Carty comes down the lane to tell us the
news.
'The Pope is dead,' he announces.
'That's right, Luke, we have a new one. John
Paul the First.'
We indulge his forgetfulness and isolation.
'He's dead too,'
Taking his pipe out to spit with emphasis.
''Twas on the radio – poisoned maybe.'
Another spit.
So, the Vatican mafia decided
The Holy Spirit had had an off day,
And got it wrong.

The first Pope to take a double name.

Albino Luciano clearly was not up to the task.

Although it is only early afternoon,

We pack up our things.

It would be disrespectful

To stay carefree

Even on distant Carty's strand

And the four-week-old Pope just dead.

Sacred Space

In the deep silence
Of the circular space,
Redolent of ritual,
And respect,
The stones embrace us
While outside everything lies fallow
In a temporary death.

Then, into the blackness,
A gleam, tentative in its intrusion,
Powerful in impact,
Creeps into the darkness
From the outer ball of light.

Silence in this sacred space
While the beam widens
To fill the chamber
For those fleeting moments.

All Souls' Day, 1999

In Killasbrogue,

On the edge of the sea,

A headstone had toppled, face down.

Names pressed into the earth,

Meeting their owners,

The cross an unnatural burden.

No need to repair

In this remote place.

But we did

To honour the dead.

Minimalist

(After Jon Fossa – Norwegian Playwright
*'My plays are about the spaces in between
people, about the presence of the invisible.'*)

'What if?'

'If what?'

'You know.'

'Know what?'

'What – if they come?'

'So what?'

'They'll know.'

'Know what?'

'What we know.'

'We don't know.'

'Know what?'

'What they think.'

'So what?'

Grief

Invisible grief

Seeps silently, insidiously

Into our humanity,

Falling drop by drop

Deep into the heart.

In time, it turns to wisdom

And causes us to love the questions

And gradually live into the answers.

Ode to Gossip

O glorious gossip,
Give us our daily spice.
Thou, which from loose lips falls
Into eager ears, precious drops
Of scandal, malice, hearsay
Laced with the ring of truth.

Uncontainable gossip;
Thou cannot live in someone's head,
Thou must be carried like winged seeds
To fall on fertile soil.

Sometimes thou growest out of control,
That cannot be undone, but rather
Flit from mouth to mouth
Altered, expanded, embellished.

Gossip art thou ever good?

Resurrection

I've just made it into heaven
Mansion 2211.
Far removed from God's right hand
Content with my lot;
Neither envy, nor jealousy here.

Three days in my new abode
Settling in with brothers Cain and Abel
And some guy called Herod.
Then the shock – downright unfair;
Back in the tomb, wrapped like a mummy;
Called forth to shut my sisters up,
To stop their endless weeping.

Back to their nagging
Do this, do that.
Two viragos forever on my back,
Forcing me to die again
To face the judgement
And maybe next time
End up in Hell!
Miracles be damned.
Dear Jesus! Why did you raise me up?

Since You Left

Since you left
Everything has faded into sepia.
What was clear now lacks definition;
I no longer see the minutiae
Which once delighted us.

I half exist,
Half-hoping you'll return
If you miss me as much as I miss you.

Or could it be
You have moved on,
Found someone else
To tease with your
Carefree ways?

The Turning

The year has turned as usual
On the cusp of the solstice
Quietly gathering momentum
Towards distant midsummer
In the inexorable rhythm of time.

White sunlight
Slants across the bareness of Winter
As majestically as into any passage tomb.
Under the mask of death
The earth reclaims its greenness
Among the tangled roots
Of last year's growth.

Today a snowdrop's green whiteness
Assures me that Winter is losing its grip
Allowing me to melt into Spring,
To abandon myself to nature's laws.
Meanwhile, days lengthen,
And my life shortens towards eternity.

Hot-wiring Granny

My Micra was stolen from right outside my
front door,
my little innocent Micra that had never
broken the law,
never as much as parked on a double yellow
line,
never been humiliated by a yellow clamp.

I hoped it was not being subjected to high
speeds
or sudden braking or that the thieves
were not destroying its spotless upholstery
with drink.
It was not used to any sort of rough
treatment.
In its ten years, it had led a sedate life of short
trips
to the supermarket, the library, the beach.
It was serviced, washed and hoovered
regularly.
It had never been asked to go on a motorway,
or carry heavy loads.
It had passed its NCT test with flying colours.
It wasn't just a car; it was my friend.
But it would not be a priority on the Garda list
of BMWs, Saabs, and Mercedes.

Two weeks passed.
Then a call came to say
it had been found safe
and reasonably well
in a car park.
It was now at the Garda Barracks
waiting to be collected.
I was glad it had not died
an ignominious death
in a ditch or a quarry
or, worse still, left as a tangled mass
of burnt out rubber and metal.
I put everything on hold
and walked the short distance
to the barracks.

The young Guard was helpful.
'Is it here?' says I.
'It is,' says he.
'Can I take it?' says I.
'I'll see,' says he.
'Thanks,' says I.
'Take a seat,' says he.
'Grand,' says I.
'You'll have to call back,' says he.
'When,' says I.
'Fifteen minutes,' says he.
'Right,' says I.
'Okay,' says he.
'Will it go?' says I.
'Sure,' says he.

'Here's the key,' says I.
'No need,' says he.
'How come?' says I.
'Hot-wired,' says he.
'What!' says I.
'Young fellas,' says he.
'How will I start it?' says I.
'Same way,' says he.
'Hot wire!' says I.
'Right,' says he.
'I don't know how,' says I.
'I'll show you,' says he.

And so, I became
A hot-wiring Granny.

Light a Candle

Our grandchildren,
eight boys, four girls,
growing up, maturing, learning.
I look at them and wonder
what can save them from
drugs, alcohol, casual sex,
invasive social media?

Now and then I light a candle,
say a prayer, and hope
with all my heart
that nothing will cripple
their beautiful lives.

Rain

He was always a secretive, sour old git,
Staring up at the sky, not doing his bit,
Predicting disaster, plagues, and floods.
Said God had told him he had regrets
About making us and all the rest,
That someday soon he'd wipe us out,
He'd start again and get it right.
Himself said we'd be spared
If we did whatever he said,
But he's almost eighty,
Gone in the head.
The sons believed him
And set to with a will.
All that talk about a race.
So, here we are in this makeshift boat,
An awkward thing that can barely float,
Day after day,
No sign of land and to make things worse,
All he does all day is sit and curse.
We're up to our ankles in vomit and muck,
The awful stench, the filth, the rows
About whose turn it is to milk the cows.

The food turns mouldy, the maggots thrive,
We don't believe we can survive.
He sits at the window, day by day,
Doesn't even bother to pray.
Then, at last, he stirs and calls for a dove,
In response to a call
From the one above.

When the bird returns with a leafy bough,
He begins to laugh:
'We're all right now.
Get ready to land, get out the plank'.
So, here we are on top of a mountain,
Soaked, sick and sore.
But himself believes
We are the saved, the chosen redeemed.

November

The oblique light of winter
Creeps into my tabernacle of memories;
Cyclical reminder of those gone,
Dust to dust,
Who made me what I am
For better, for worse.

Faces have blurred into sepia
But the timbre of their voices
Remains under layers of invading sounds,
Between the notes of life's music
Lodged somewhere safe from obliteration.

Their silent soundings
Compel me to pray:
'Lux aeterna luceat eis'.

Snow Woman

We built a snow woman
In the front garden.
We named her Lulu.
She had Christmas candle lips,
Magnificent hips,
Courgette green eyes,
Match-stick eyelashes.
A flowing red skirt,
A red and white T-shirt.
A feathered hat
Made her a magnificent creature.
A very correct neighbour
Demanded her immediate dispatch.
We said:
'Lulu will die a natural death
Like we all hope for'.
Lulu lived a week and two days,
Then passed away quietly
In the early hours of a thawing dawn.
The first snow woman in our parts.

The Far Side

The far side of the town was Indian country,
Where women stood smoking at back doors,
Shouting abuse across weedy gardens,
Criss-crossed by sagging clothes lines;
Tyres hanging from stunted bushes.

The kids had nits, worms and snotty noses.
The men checked form in raggy English
newspapers.
The school attendance officer,
The Guards frequent callers.
A postman was a rare sight.
No priest ever called on first Fridays.

Some kept grey pigs or scrawny hens
That rooted and scratched
In a hopeless search.
Others had ferrets for rabbit hunting,
Or skinny greyhounds that never raced.
Cats were common property.

There even was a house of bad repute

Where the granny ruled

From a large armchair in the front room.

Her daughters and their daughters

Were at the disposal of merchant seamen

From Glasgow or Liverpool.

It was said no local man ever crossed their

threshold.

Transcendence

A precious moment
In mid-winter
Ignited by the mystery of the Christ child,
Shreds my pride,
Melts my resistance,
Leaves me open to the divine.
I rise above the mundane,
Quit trying to make sense of things.

A faith greater than love
Makes the impossible believable,
Relieves me of the burden of proof
In a world driven mad by logic.

Líonta

Is minic a chaith tú amach
Na líonta láidre
Chun saibhreas na mara
A tharraingt isteach,
Fíor-bhuíochas i do bhéal.

Ach faraor, sciob an fharraige chrúalach
Mo ghrá uaim ró-luath
An oíche uafásach sin.

Cá raibh tú, a Thiarna,
Agus mo laoch a bhá?
Ní raibh tú ag tabhairt aire
Do mo ghrá,
Tusa atá mar Rí
Ar gach uile ní.

Anois a stór, tá tú curtha cois cladaigh,
Líon gorm mar chlúdach ar do uaigh
Chun na bláthanna bréige
A shábháil ar an aimsir.

Acknowledgements

I wish to acknowledge the encouragement and support of the Salthill Active Retirement Writers' group where my love of writing was encouraged under the initial tutorship of Máire Holmes.

My involvement with the Write-on group in Westside Resource Centre has allowed my work to flourish in an atmosphere of creative nourishment. Some of the poems in this collection and many of my short stories were published in *The Write-on Anthology 2020*.

I also wish to thank Frank Fahy without whose encouragement and support these poems would have simply died on my computer – he saved them from oblivion.

The Write-on group wish to thank Galway City Council Arts Office for funding towards this project.

About the Author

Anne McManus (née Henry) was born in Sligo town, where her imagination was nurtured by books, music, the sea, local history, and the run of a large garden.

She qualified as a home economics teacher, and later graduated from NUIG with a degree in German and English.

Married to Ray, they have four children and twelve grandchildren.

Her inspiration comes from the observation of the quirkiness of daily life, the flashes of humanity in ordinary events, and the unexpected.

Index

46321266R00031

Printed in Poland
by Amazon Fulfillment
Poland Sp. z o.o., Wrocław